Healing Broken Machines

Dedication

I dedicate this book to all the men and women that grew up during the 60's and 70's, a time when children were abused physically and psychologically by both their parents and state officials and all legally too. I pray that those of you that were victims during this time period will find a way to the cross where Jesus can heal you of all your pain.

Forward

This book may be offensive to some, but if they have the guts to read it to the end, they will find that there truly is redemption, and that the God I serve, Jesus, is the redeemer of souls. Take a trip with me through the life of fictionaly character based on a man that society has thrown away as non-redeemable, but Jesus found a way to bring grace, mercy and peace into the picture. Jesus can save any man or woman from the pits of hell. All we have to do is repent of our sins and follow Him.

This book is a fictional work aimed at crossing the bridge of reality and changing your life. If you are a minister of God's Word that goes into the prisons, I challenge you to take a second look at how you approach the men in these prisons. Rather than treating them as guys in prison being ministered to, try treating them as missionaries on a foreign field that have special needs. You will see a huge increase in the movement of the church within those prison or jail walls.

Remember, you are not trying to re-create the organized church you came from but rather a true movement of the Holy Spirit that can transform even the worst psychotic ever created by God. Yes, God created the psychotic too, just like He did you and He loves them just as much and will set them free if we only have the guts to deliver the message. Do you sir, madam, have the guts? Read this book and find out how powerful of a God we really have.

Copyright 2012
Gary Mallett

ISBN 978-1-329-62580-8

Table of Contents

Chapter 1   Santee California 1970
Chapter 2   Los Angeles California 1971 – 1978
Chapter 3   1979
Chapter 4   1980
Chapter 5   Bonnie and Clyde 1981
Chapter 6   1984
Chapter 7   This Trial
Chapter 8   Death Row
Chapter 9   2008
Chapter 10 2010

Healing Broken Machines

Have you ever wondered what causes a man with an IQ of 140 to become a broken machine with-in society? A psychopathic criminal and killer!

I have, as I am housed in what I refer to as Satan's Castle (maximum security prison), and it is full of broken machines just like me.

Many of these men were state raised, just like I was, and although they belong where they are at, if society had dealt with them differently when they were youngsters, many would not be here today, and many of their victims would not be victims.

I live in a prison and will continue to do so until the day I die. I am a broken machine.

The people in this story are not real but be assured that every vile crime described in this book has actually happened to many people throughout the years and that the young boy described within is real but will never be named.

This is a sad story of how our juvenile system so often creates criminal monsters and that the true redemption of souls comes only through Jesus Christ our Lord and Savior.

Chapter 1
Santee California 1970

My parents divorced when I was six years old. I had two brothers, and two sisters, Ronnie, Greg, Tanya and Kira.

Two of us went with my dad while the youngest three (Greg, Tanya and Kira) stayed with our mom. We moved to Santee California where dad's parents owned a home that they allowed my dad and us two boys to live.

We spent the next several years as a somewhat normal middle class American family.

My dad was an insurance broker and remarried a woman who had a girl that was a couple of years younger than I by the name of Pat. Pat and I got along really well as she looked up to me as her defender.

I got my butt kicked a pile of times by my older brother, protecting her.

When I was around ten, my dad went into a new business. I didn't know at the time what he was doing but I knew that it was illegal. I later found out that he was running guns for the mob.

It was during this time period that my dad started getting physically abusive to all of us kids. He would have these fits of madness where he would take large extension cords and baseball bats and beat the hell out of both myself and my brother.

He never touched Pat as her mother would not have tolerated that but she would not defend us boys as we were not hers, oh and let's not forget that I had tried to poison her a few times too.

We were far from being perfect angels but the beatings that dad laid upon us were horrific. My arms, ribs, legs, hand, feet, had all been broken in the past 2 years by dad, not to mention the multiple contusions all over my body most of the time.

This went on for a couple of years. One night I came home from hanging out with my friends. I was supposed to have been home for dinner and washed dishes but had blown it off in order to hang with my friends and was about 2 hours late. I came in the door and my dad was all the way up in my face, accusing me of being on drugs.

I had never done any drugs in my life but I was a bit tipsy from alcohol. Dad started yelling at me and then suddenly his right fist came smashing into my face, knocking me into the TV and smashing it into a hundred pieces. Then, because the TV was broken, he really got mad and picked up a ball bat and began to hit me over and over again. First, he hit my arm, breaking it in three places, then, he broke my other arm.

He then got mad at himself for breaking my bones and began to cry and ask for my forgiveness. I tried to make him happy and tell him it was ok, and then he got mad again because he said that I was lying.

He picked up an orange extension cord and began to beat me senseless, hitting me so many times that I came to a point where I simply could not move anymore and just wished I were dead.

My dad took me to my Grand-ma's house that night, so that she could set my broken arms in a casts and clean all of my wounds.

My Grand-ma was a Registered Nurse working at the local emergency room, so she knew exactly what to do to get me on the road to recovery.

I didn't think about it back when I was a kid, but what the hell was going on in Granny's head to cover up these horrid crimes. I am willing to bet that if I were ever able to find out the truth, it would be to the effect of my Grand Father was an abuser and she was the abused, and the relationship continued on with my dad and her, therefore, in spite of her profession, she was submissive and covered his tracks for him.

One day at school a boy challenged me to a fight. He was huge in comparison to my skinny runt self, so I pulled a David and Goliath on him. I picked up a rock and chucked it as hard as I could and hit him dead between the eyes.

He stood there for a moment and then blood began to roll down his forehead. Then he simply dropped like a rag doll, knocked out cold. I expected cheering from the crowd that had gathered but instead they all seemed to want to attack and injure me.

This kid had a lot of friends and on my way home from school that day the fights began. I was in the school office due to the rock in head incident and they determined that I had been simply playing and thrown the rock in the wrong direction and accidentally hit the boy.

I was not punished at all, but wanted to stay in the office and have my dad pick me up because I knew that trouble was awaiting me outside.

His friends outside, didn't buy the story I had given the school officials, as they knew me all too well. I tried to plan my escape from the campus in a route of least resistance, going out the front, past the buses, down this little trail and around the back of my house.

I got about 10 yards and they were on my like a pack of wolves. I snatched antennae off of a car and began to swing it like a sword. I was swinging my antennae and dancing around hitting one of the boys with every swing. They were quickly scattering at the onslaught I presented to them.

Then I saw a ball bat and picked it up, chasing all of them down the street, but not before I had inflicted some pretty serious wounds upon their heads.

Yeah baby I was now the ultimate champion fighter of our entire school and dad would now celebrate with me rather than kick my ass.

Surprise, when I got home, the police were at the door talking to my dad. They said that I had attacked those boys and beat them with no mercy.

One of them was in the hospital due to a head injury and another due to internal bleeding and massive welts all over his body, from my make shift sword.

The police questioned me and determined that I was in need of psychiatric assistance but had not committed any crime. They recommended that my dad seek proper assistance for me.

The police left and as soon as the door closed, his hand swung and I caught a stiff left hook in the jaw.

When I woke up, I was being kicked and bludgeoned with an axe handle. Once he was finished, I crawled to the corner and hid under a pile of old carpeting, in hopes that he would forget I was there and pick on someone else for awhile.

During this time I became very rebellious and began to act out in many ways. I was getting into fights at school almost daily, breaking into garages and stealing beer at night.

Heck, we even learned the underground drainage in our city so that we could steal beer out of the back of the bars and drop it through a man hole where our compadres would be waiting for the goods.

One afternoon, I got drunk on some stolen booze and was arrested for breaking out the lights at the school with a basketball. They called it malicious mischief.

While I was at the police station they noticed the bruises all over my body and began to question me about them. I told the officers the truth and they took pictures and told me not to worry as my dad would never do this to me again.

After I had been at the police station for many hours, a woman came and got me and drove me to a home in East San Diego where I was placed in a foster home. She told me that they would contact my mom and have her come get me as soon as possible.

My brother and I had only seen our mom maybe once or twice a year since the divorce so we did not know her very well but I was sure she would come and get us, because she said she would, right?

There were five kids at this foster home and at first the people seemed nice enough but all of the kids acted scared all of the time and that made me uncomfortable.

Four days later a lady showed up out of the blue and told me that I was going home. I walked outside with her only to discover that my dad was there to pick me up. I was scared to death, here we go again, these people won't help me, and instead they just keep making it worse.

He told me how much he loved me and that everything was going to change at home.

Everything was cool for a couple of weeks and then all hell broke loose. My dad snapped one night because his wife locked him out of the bedroom, and began to beat both my brother and me with the extension cord again. The welts that those things leave are huge and ugly and when I awakened the next day, I had welts all over my body.

My brother had a broken arm and welts too. More importantly, Pat, my step sister was also among the wounded, with a broken leg.

Dad had now crossed a line that he wouldn't have before.

My brother and I knew that we were in deep shit and began trying to contact our mom and even spoke to an uncle about the possibility of living with his family.

This physically tormentive abuse went on for another six months, daily beatings, until one day the FBI came to the door and arrested my dad on charges of interstate transport of stolen guns.

Wow, what an experience that was. My dog, Bimbo, began growling. My brother and I lived in a makeshift bedroom in the garage, so we were separated 12 from the house. Our dog alerted us to the presence of something or someone outside. I got out of bed and snuck around the back and saw a team of federal agents with riot gear on, surrounding our house.

My brother was right behind me and we climbed the hill out back so that we could watch in safety, as these guys looked like they were going to do a full on attack of the house.

We didn't have cell phones back in those days, so we couldn't call and warn dad of what was going on outside.

We could shoot rocks from our sling-shot and break a window in an attempt to warn him though, and so we did. I had a wrist rocket stashed in our underground fort and Ronnie was an ace shot with it. Ronnie pulled back the wrist rocket and let go, the rock sailed through the air like a bullet and broke our dad's bedroom window.

The light came on and then all hell broke loose. The Feds kicked in both the front and back doors and went in like gang busters ready for world war three.

Dad had turned his bedroom light on so we were able to see everything happening in the room. When the FBI came into the bedroom, guns were blazing in both directions.

We watched helplessly as our step mother and sister were brutally murdered by the FBI. Yes I said murdered. They were still asleep when the bullets started flying, and never even awoke before they had their bodied riddled with bullets.

Our dad was wounded but would live. Two FBI were also wounded during the raid.

They took him away and he eventually got sentenced to ten years in federal prison. I wished they had given him life as I never wanted to see him again, ever.

My brother and I were also taken into custody. They split us up and took me to a foster home. I don't know where they took my brother as I did not see him again for many years.

I was told that my mom would be coming to pick me up in a few days. Days turned into weeks and weeks into months and mom never showed up.

I was in the same foster home that I had been in the first time, and one night the foster dad took me on what he called a day trip.

He took me up into the hills to hike and while we were in the hills, he began to touch my legs and then my groin area. I tried to fight back but was only a 12 year old kid, weighing all of 110 lbs. He was a full grown man of 200 lbs.

I never had a chance. He brutally beat and raped me over and over again. When he was done my anal cavity was bleeding, so he performed his sick form of nursing upon me and stopped it from bleeding anymore. Yeah this foster care thing is even worse than at home with dad.

It was 1970 and child advocacy had not yet been invented, so, when I tried to tell my social worker, she told me that I was just making it up, like I had when I accused my dad of beating me.

She simply did not believe me and dismissed the idea out of cuff as though it was just my vivid imagination and therefore she never heard me. That would never happen today however in those days it was the norm.

I was truly on my own and thus made a decision to run away and find my mom. I knew she lived in an exclusive section of Los Angeles called Toluca Lake, so if I could only get there, she would save me from all of this insanity.

I placed all of my clothing into a sleeping bag I found in the garage and walked up to the freeway and began hitchhiking to L.A. where I thought my mom was, Toluca Lake.

I stuck my thumb out and it was only a few minutes before my first ride pulled over.

There were two people in the car, a man and a woman. They offered me a ride to the next town and I accepted.

After I had gotten into the car the woman lit up a funny smelling cigarette and handed it to me. I didn't smoke yet but accepted it and we passed the thing around.

I began to feel weird and asked her what this was. She told me it was marijuana laced with a drug called PCP, and asked if I liked it.

I said yes and then she asked if I would like to come over to their house and smoke some more.

Sure why not, I am feeling pretty good. I had never smoked anything nor done any type of drugs or alcohol.

I had just turned thirteen and had actually lived a fairly sheltered life.

We got to their house and began to get stoned out of our minds. I was so high on this stuff that I thought I was walking sideways and became extremely disoriented but was laughing and having a blast at the same time.

A little while later they broke out some booze and somewhere along the line they gave me a tab of 15 LSD.

Wow what a trip I was on. Everything was psychedelic, trails everywhere and I was seeing things that were really crazy. One of the things I saw was a Cyclops with a woman's body and it was naked.

The Cyclops began to have sex with me and then pretty soon there was another beast that looked like a lion with horns and it too was demanding sex.

I went along with it as I was so high that I had no grasp of reality at all. We had the wildest time one could imagine, it was like being in a wild sex show with crazy animals from some movie. I got bucked, sucked, pulled on, and turned in every direction, for the first time I was having enjoyable sex, wow, was this even real? Or am I just hallucinating?

I awakened in a field under some trees, naked, cold and wet. I was naked and there were people standing around looking at me, laughing and talking in quiet voices.

I scrambled around trying to find something to cover my nakedness but couldn't, finally a lady handed me her sweater and I wrapped it around myself.

About that time a police cruiser pulled up and I was placed under arrest and taken to the San Diego Juvenile Hall where I was booked in on run-away and indecent exposure.

I told the case workers what had transpired but did not know any names or even where these people lived.

They had apparently dumped me in the field passed out.

The case workers didn't believe me anywise and they were convinced that I was a habitual liar that just made up stories about beatings and sexual molestation.

I would have need of taking pictures for them to believe it and even then I doubt they would have.

I spent the next three months in juvenile hall and actually found some solace there as I was treated like a human being and no one sexually assaulted me.

One day they came and got me and told me that my mom was there to pick me up. Apparently they had found her.

Chapter 2
Los Angeles California 1971 - 1978

My mom was waiting for me in the visiting room. We went out and got into her car, where her boyfriend was waiting. She introduced us, his name was Ralph.

He seemed like an ok guy as we had fun talking, joking and laughing on the way to where they lived in Toluca Lake, California.

At first, things were pretty good at mom's house. She had a two bedroom apartment and my little brother, and sister Kira, was there too.

I had never had an opportunity to get to know them as they had lived with mom all of these years. Greg was five years younger than I, and Kira was a year younger than he, so I was the new live in baby sitter.

I got enrolled in junior high and tried to fit in as the new kid.

Mom bought me a bunch of new clothes, so I was styling all of the time, which of course helped with my social life.

It wasn't long though until I was getting into fights at school, and got suspended several times.

I always hated bullies and had observed this 9th grader that was strong arming the nerds for their lunches. I took offense at these actions and decided to act upon my impulses. I walked up behind him and poured a pint of chocolate milk over his head. He turned in both surprise and anger and I cold cocked him and then pounced on him and began to beat the holy day light out of him. A couple of teachers pulled me off and I did not resist. The crowd was cheering, so although I was about to get suspended, I was a hero and would return in a few days as a triumphant hero.

I was taken to the vice principals office, Mr. Hunter. I waited outside of his office for about 30 minutes and then was ushered in to see this crazy old geezer with a huge leather strap full of holes in his hand. Yes corporal punishment was still legal in schools.

He began talking about how fighting was not acceptable in his school and that if I liked to fight, I would meet with his strap and get a beating.

I told the old geezer to go screw him-self; he wasn't using that thing on me. Mr. Hunter was aghast; I don't think any kid had ever spoken to him like this before. He then told me to get out of his office and go home; I was suspended for three days.

I hitch hiked down to Santa Monica pier where I learned to fish and got exposed to some of the wild side of the beach, down at Venice.

There were some really strange folks on that beach. If you have never been to Venice beach, you have been deprived in life. This is a wild and crazy place where anything goes. There were vendors of all sorts, selling everything from hot dogs, hippy paraphernalia, to clothes, surfboards. There were performers of all sorts, mimes, clowns, vampires in bikinis, freaks, geeks, acid freaks and horror shows.

Whatever one wanted drug wise, was of course readily available.

One of the people I met was a guy named Pastor Dick and he kept telling me about this Jesus dude and how he could help me straighten out my life.

I liked Pastor Dick so I listened to him and one day was invited over to his house. He fed me and gave me some new clothes and then took me to a church where folks were singing and clapping their hands and all of them would scream out in some strange language, and yet others would speak out real loud in old English as though they were God speaking, saying things like, "Thus saith the Lord God of Israel, I am the provider of my people, the healer of the nations, the creator of all things, I AM".

They prayed over one another and people were falling down on the ground and they would just lay there and twitch. I thought that all of this was a bit strange but they were nice to me and kept telling me some dude named Jesus loved me.

I had known a dude named Jesus back in Santee, and he was a Mexican hippy that was always higher than a kite.

This Jesus they were talking about certainly had to be a different Jesus.

Mom worked a lot so she was not around to keep an eye on me. I was supposed to be watching my little brother and sister at night while she went to work on her 2nd job.

I did not like her job though as it was not one where she went into a building and worked but rather she was picked up each night in a limo and there was always a different man in it. Sometimes the driver, Dan, would come into the house and give me a dollar for babysitting, other times they would just wait for her in the car.

She was doing what she felt she had too in order to provide a home and food for us kids.

I had gotten suspended from school so many times for fighting that they eventually expelled me. I was persona non grata from the Los Angeles School District.

They mailed my mom a letter telling her this, but I snagged it out of the mail, so she wouldn't know.

This gave me the ability to hitch down to the beach and hang out with my friends, every day.

By this time I had started smoking pot on a regular basis, and was selling it on the board walk to all the freaks of Venice.

I started out slinging dime bags but soon stepped up to larger amounts. I had a knack for selling people on a product and making them happy with their purchases, so they kept coming back to me.

I also learned a bit about business during this time. In the pot slinging business,

I had need of giving people credit at times, in order to get the sales that I needed.

As is life, some folks don't like to pay. I quickly gained a reputation of not being a guy in whom one wants to burn on a deal.

The first time a guy stiffed me, here is what happened. George owed me $50 for some smoke that I had fronted him. He publicly made a statement saying, "I'm not paying that punk, and he can't do a dam thing about it".

An associate told me about this and I had to either act or go out of business.

I found George on the Santa Monica Pier, where I had been told he would be.

I walked up and quietly asked him to pay me the money. He hee hawed around trying to avoid answering me. I had a 6" crow bar in my pocket and I pulled it out and beat the hell out of him right there on the pier.

When I left him, he was breathing but had several broken limbs. I then walked away and went back to Venice, where word spread quickly and I never had a nonpayment issue again.

One day my friend Pastor Dick saw me, and asked if I would like to go on a camp out with him and some of his friends. I figured they were going to be a bunch of those Jesus freaks and figured that would be safe enough, so went.

I don't know if I had a sign on my forehead that said rape and beat me or what when I was a kid, but once again that was going to be my fate.

Pastor Dick and two of his friends took me up to Big Bear Lake and at first we had fun cruising on a boat and fishing but later that night the molestation began and I was the prize of the party.

The three men repeatedly had anal intercourse with me and forced me, with a gun, to give them blow jobs over a four day period.

I was held prisoner, actually being locked into a basement at night, fed cold oatmeal and water, and beaten with a whip while handcuffed to the walls.

It was crazy, these morons would come down to the basement where they had a bed set up and they would rape and beat me, over and over again.

I was attached to a metal wall fixture with a chain and handcuffs. They fed me food as though I were a dog, in a bowl on the floor with a cup of water.

I thought that they were going to kill me. I awakened to find them all sleeping. I had gotten my hands on a bobby pin and used it to pick the lock on the handcuffs, and slipped out the door of the cabin.

I began to run and run and run falling, tripping, and stumbling my way through the darkness of the hills I found myself in. I had no idea where I was but I knew that I had to stay away from any roads until I felt it was safe. I stumbled through the darkness of the mountains barefoot, tired, hurting, and suffering from what would now be known as post traumatic stress disorder.

I was hungry and thirsty, so I approached an empty cabin and broke a window to get in and check out what might be in the cupboards.

I found food and a warm bed so settled in for the night and after a shower in the morning, I went out to the road and I stuck my thumb out and began to hitch a ride.

A guy picked me up and apparently I looked a bit tattered and scared so he asked me what was wrong.

I told him everything that had transpired and broke down crying. This guy promised me that he would take me to San Bernardino and we could go to the police and report the abduction and molestation.

We got to San Bernardino and he basically kicked me out the door on the steps of the police station.

I went inside and told the police what had transpired. At first they acted as though they were going to help me.

A lady social worker showed up and took me to a hospital where they did test on me to determine if I had indeed been raped.

I required several stitches in my rectum and spent the next two days in the hospital.

Then they told me that it would be my word against a pastor, and that the DA would not prosecute such a case due to it being unwinnable.

They contacted my mom and she refused to come and get me, saying that I was incorrigible and that she could no longer provide a home for me.

I was then taken to San Bernardino Juvenile Hall where I was booked for incorrigibility.

Worse yet, while I was being booked the police told all of the 23 staff about my being raped, and did so in front of other kids.

The word was out that I was a punk (punk in those days meant a guy who had been force raped and was too much of a bitch to do anything about it) which meant I was either going to be raped again or have to do some serious ass whooping.

I spent the next six months in that juvenile hall. I had not committed any crime, in fact was the victim of such, but was treated as a criminal by the system.

I was incorrigible which meant uncontrollable. The cop's big mouth at the time of my booking caused me to have a punk jacket on me so the fight was just getting going.

My third night at the facility three older boys came into my cell and tried to rape me. I had a pillow case full of books and used it as a weapon to fight them off successfully.

I was going to have to overcome this punk jacket and make a name for myself that would make it where no one would want to mess with me. Over the next few weeks I caught those three boys one by one, alone, and beat the holy crap out of them. Each time, I would get into trouble and be placed in isolation for three days for fighting.

As soon as they let me out of isolation, I would go catch another one and beat him too.

I quickly gained a reputation of being a serious fighter.

This only perpetuated the problem though, as now, all of the other fighters wanted a piece of me to see if they could kick my ass.

The next several months were a blur of fights, courts and trips to the psych hospital where I was being evaluated.

The evaluation stated that I had an IQ in the top 10% in the nation and that I had a tendency towards a sociopathic and psychopathic personality. My interpretation of that was that I was very bright but had no remorse when I did something wrong. Well, these pricks that had beat and raped me through the years did not have any remorse either and nobody gave a rat's ass about what had happened. So what did they expect me to be like?

I was finally sent to a boy's ranch where I was told I would have to stay until I was eighteen years old.

Everyone else there had committed crimes to get there, and most would be released within a year.

I had been raped, that was my crime and I was going to be there for four years. What's wrong with that picture?

The boy's ranch was certainly better than juvenile hall but I was still locked up and really had not done anything to get there.

I had a real attitude about that and rebelled consistently at every turn.

It was during this time that I learned a very important lesson. The lesson was that not only could they lock up your body but if you pushed things to hard they could take your mind also.

There was a boy by the name of Larry that was a very rebellious lad. This kid was hyper to the bone. He had and I don't care attitude about life.

One day they came and took Larry to the local mental institution. He returned about a month later and was like a robot.

He acted like a guy that was a mindless empty body. He did manage to tell me one day though that he had been used as a guinea pig for electro shock therapy.

I never forgot this as I now knew that if you pushed the system to hard, they could literally take your mind from you.

The owners of the ranch were Christians, so one of the requirements was that we had to attend church three times a week.

I had a real phobia of church and Christians due to my experiences with Pastor Dick. He was a Christian and he and his friends had brutally raped me.

I consistently refused to go to church with them, I simply did not trust them and thought that their religion was a fake and fraud that would do nothing but suck me in and hurt me.

As a result of my rebellion, I was always on restriction and not allowed any privileges. The owner had his favorites and they were allowed to go into town to mingle with girls and go bowling, but I was never allowed to go.

While the others were in town one of the counselors in the place would remain with me. He would not allow me to watch TV or anything as that was a privilege that I was not allowed.

The counselor began to use privileges such as the watching of TV to lure me into sexual acts.

He would sell me TV time for a hand job and would get me high if I gave him a blow job.

He was just like all the other Christians I had met, a molester. I tried to tell the owner but was rebuffed with, "I've read your file and you have a history of making false accusations like this, if you continue doing so I will have to send you back to juvenile hall."

You must remember, I was only 14 years old at this point and had been brutally molested multiple times by people in whom one is supposed to be able to trust and now I had one forcing me to perform sexual acts on him in lieu of pay, making me a prostitute for the Christian boy's home counselor.

And they wondered why I had attitude, hmmmm.

Looking back on everything that happened back then, I must wonder. How come there is so much child molestation within the church and nobody seems to be addressing the issue?

In today's churches they are able to run back ground checks, etc on workers but that only stops the ones that have been caught before, not the offender that has never been caught.

The Catholic Church has been hit by huge scandals of sexual molestation and it has cost them multitudes of millions of dollars.

The protestant church though, has done very little to prevent or address these issues and they do exist, do not fool yourself.

I personally was molested by ministers in at least two churches and a Christian ministry while growing up and nobody ever even acknowledged it.

They turned me into a sexual whore. After about eleven months in this place, I decided to run away.

The ranch was way out in the boondocks so I stole a horse and rode it to the city of Escondido, California, which was about a 20 mile ride.

It was dark and we were traversing some pretty rugged country, but we made it fine before morning.

Once in town, I tied the horse up to a parking pole at a Denny's and hitch hiked to L.A.

I was now fifteen years old and free, hallelujah.

Or so I thought. I met a gal named Phyllis who helped me out by taking me into her home and feeding me. She set me up with a job escorting older women to parties.

At first it seemed fun and glamorous but I soon found myself in a position where I was servicing these ladies sexually for money.

I spent about three months doing this and was making great money.

I started using cocaine and quickly became addicted. One day just flowed into the next in a blur of parties and lots of money flowing freely in all directions.

One day I was hanging out at the mall and saw a car where the keys had been left in it. I stole the car and headed down the road.

The only problem was that I did not know how to drive, and this was an Opal GT stick shift. I had at least driven an automatic before but never a stick shift.

I was screeching and grinding all over the place. As I came around a corner I hit another car and was scared so took off at a very high rate of speed.

A motorcycle cop had seen me commit the hit and run and began to follow me. I was on Ventura Blvd in the San Fernando Valley and began to speed trying to get away from the cop. Pretty quickly I had cops all over the place, we were doing 70+ down side streets but somehow managed to keep the car on the road. Somehow, I ended up on the San Diego freeway headed into Santa Monica and we were now doing 100+ miles per hour.

The chase was getting really crazy. I had cops all around me and a helicopter in the air above.

We raced down the San Diego Freeway at 120 mph. Cop cars were following me and they were blocking off on-ramps so that cars could not enter the freeway in front of me, coinciding with getting cars onto the off-ramps. They were obviously clearing the road off.

Towards the end of the chase there were two police cars in front, two alongside and two behind me.

They had slowed me down to about 70 mph by boxing me in such a way. One of the cops in front of me did a maneuver that caused me to slam into the center divider.

As I hit the cement divider, one of the cops behind me rammed into me and his car flipped over the center divider.

I was briefly stunned by my head slamming into the steering wheel. When I came too, and rose up my head, there must have been twenty guns pointing at me, and cops screaming "get out of the car".

I was beaten, arrested and put in the back of a police car handcuffed behind my back. A cop got into the back seat with me and put a gun to my head and told me that I would not make it to the police station alive. I believed him.

The cops then drove me to Rampart police station and parked across the street.

They got me out of the car and took my handcuffs off. They then told me to walk over to the police station. I was no dummy and understood that if I took that walk, they were going to shoot me and claim I had tried to escape.

What I did instead was to lie down on the ground spread eagle and refused to move.

They beat the hell out of me right there in the street and then took me to jail.

At last I am finally in jail for actually committing a crime.

This was my first experience at Los Angeles Central Juvenile Hall.

This place was a zoo. I was a white boy and therefore a major minority in the place, gangs abounded and the staff could care less what happened to a kid.

I was getting my first experience in the jungle with the wild animals.

In order to survive, I joined a white supremacist gang and proceeded to become one of the baddest boys in the place.

I quickly gained a reputation that if someone screwed with me that I would stab, maim or kill.

I was not there to play games so if you wanted a piece of me, you better come prepared to do it right.

I had made up my mind that NO ONE was ever going to sexually abuse me again, and I would kill anyone who tried to.

I started a protection racket where those that were weak could come under my covering and I would protect them from all of the animals, for a price of course. In return the boys would do my bidding, have money placed on my books, have their sisters visit them and let me get alone with these hot babes, where they could give me a hand/blow job. Hey a guy has got to get what he can in a situation like this.

I truly cared about the boys under my protection and was perfectly willing to kill anyone that attempted to harm them in any manner.

I had been charged with Grand Theft Auto, Evading the police, and Assault with a deadly weapon with intent to do great bodily harm upon a peace officer. I was sentenced to the CYA (California Youth Authority) until the age of twenty one. Upon arrival at CYA I was evaluated and sent to a place called YTS (Youth Training Center) or more commonly known as "Gladiator School". The kids that were sent to this institution were the worst of the worst and it was widely known that this was a place that kids were sent to prepare them for prison.

No one had any intentions of trying to bring rehabilitation to me or any of the other kids incarcerated there.

This was a place full of gang bangers, thieves, murderers, armed robbers, and rapist. Nobody gave a dam what became of the animals.

The very first day that I was at YTS they placed me in a cell block that was 99% black and I was in deep trouble.

These guys looked at me like I was dessert being served on a platter and they were going to eat me.

I went to the so called counselors (in reality they were cops or rather zoo keepers) and asked to be transferred to a tank where there were more white guys but was told, "you tried to kill a cop, deal with it prick".

I knew I was in deep trouble here. I took a sock and loaded it with soap to create a weapon and walked up to a guy and began to beat the living hell out of him right in front of the cops in hopes that they would put me in isolation.

It worked. They moved me to administrative segregation for the next two months.

I felt bad for the poor guy that I whooped on, but hey, he was simply in the wrong place at the wrong time. When they finally let me out of segregation, I was placed on a block that was predominantly whites and Mexicans.

I spent the next two years living in this zoo and saw a boy's head cut off, more than nineteen murders, multitudes of rapes, so many boys stabbed or beat that I lost count, and lived through two riots where the entire block was taken over and then stormed by police with rubber bullets and bean bags fired from shotguns.

Never once in my entire time in this institution did anyone even attempt to act like they were trying to rehabilitate or help us boys.

The cops were there simply to watch the animals and try to keep them from killing one another.

During this time we started a gang named Lowriding Nazis which later became one of the largest prison gangs in the California prison system.

I remember the day we started it. The whites and the Mexicans were seriously outnumbered by the blacks and had need of linking hearts in order to survive.

A guy named David Lewis, Gary James, Albert Garcia, Juan Esparza and myself sat down at a picnic bench in the yard and forged out a deal to merge our troops and go whoop some ass on the blacks.

A riot ensued and the Low-riding Nazis were birthed.

Today the Low-riding Nazis are predominantly a white prison gang but in the beginning it was multiracial in that we had whites, Mexicans, Central Americans, and a Puerto Rican.

During the riot, I got stabbed in the chest and was sent to the hospital via ambulance. I spent two weeks in the hospital recovering.

While there, I met a nurse's aide that was a really pretty gal. I managed to get her into bed with me and she fell in love.

I of course used this relationship to do what I did best, run. Early on in my troubles with the law I had been nick named Rabbit, by a probation officer. All of the cops and employees at San Bernardino Juvenile Hall had called me this daily as I held the record for escape attempts with 8 tries at the fence and one successful escape where I was caught about 5 blocks away.

Her name was Lupe and she was a nineteen year old ½ Mexican/White girl that had a body to die for.

I talked her into assisting me in escaping.

I was handcuffed to the bed and there was a guard outside the door of my room.

The guard often wandered down the hall way to talk to nurses, use the restroom, etc.

Lupe got a girlfriend of hers to seduce the guard and while she was doing him in a utility closet, Lupe came into my room with handcuff keys and turned me loose.

She had a car so we simply walked to the parking lot and drove away.

We drove to L.A. and I linked up with some gang bangers I had met in YTS.

It was a motorcycle club called the Mongolians.

I spent the next six months in East L.A. committing burglaries, robberies and committed my first rape and murder while I prospected for the club.

I earned a Harley by doing what I was told and became the youngest person ever to become a full patched member of the club.

I was barely eighteen by a few days when they patched me up.

Rape and murder? Yes, rape and murder.

I was out with some friends at the beach and saw that bastard, Pastor Dick, with a woman.

When we approached, he introduced her as his wife. I acted as though nothing bad had ever happened between us and invited myself over to their house for some dinner.

We were in the living room of Pastor Dick's house and I picked up a baseball bat and hit him in the head, knocking him out.

I then made his wife stand in the corner while I tied him up with some rope I had found in the kitchen. When he awakened from his nap, I proceeded to rape his wife both vaginally and anally, beating her about the head as I did so.

Then while he was watching, I slit her throat with a razor knife and let her blood pour out all over him.

I then proceeded to rape him anally, while he was hanging upside down, with the baseball bat. He begged me throughout the rapes, asking me to forgive him as Jesus had already done so.

I told him, "Jesus forgives, I don't" as I cut off his genitals and then left him to lie there and bleed to death slowly with his genitals hanging from his mouth.

I went out to the San Fernando Valley from there and went on a two week drunk. I do not remember much of what happened during that time but when I awakened from my daze, I was back in jail.

I had apparently been arrested for drunk in public and of course escape.

They sent me back to YTS where I hit the yard already a feared leader.

We created a protection racket and also began to run heroin into the facility.

My Mongolian brothers were supplying the drugs and ensuring that I had visits every week. We paid off guards to bring the heroin in and then distributed it mostly on credit for double the normal price.

This was a very lucrative operation that created a small empire for those of us in leadership.

I would say that 90% of all contraband that comes into a detention facility is smuggled in by a staff member.

It is a major issue throughout the United States, even today, as many corrections officers make double or even triple their yearly salary by smuggling contraband.

Chapter 3
1979

I finally turned twenty one and they had to let me go. Look out world, ready or not, here I come.

I decided to take my act on the road and stole a motor-home and pulled my Harley behind it on a trailer.

There were four of us traveling together, my girl Lupe, and a Mongolian brother named Cutthroat, and his girl Erica.

We traveled all over the country driving from California to Florida, then up to New York and over to Denver.

Everywhere we went it was a rolling crime wave.

Back in those days there were no computers so as long as we kept moving the cops were following a cold scent.

We would usually enter a city starting on Friday night. We typically would have mapped out our crime spree in advance so that by Monday morning we were a couple of hundred miles away.

As winter hit we decided to go south and ended up in Texas. We found a place called Padre Island on the Gulf coast that was a non-stop party.

We spent about a month right on the beach living in our motor-home and riding our Harleys around the area.

We had made some serious cash up north and were now enjoying the fruits of our labor.

We were of course flying our Mongolians MC patches whenever we rode our bikes.

One night we were in a small town by the name of Corpus Christi Texas. This was a small berg on the coast of the Gulf of Mexico. We were hanging out at a bar and a group of bikers pulled up flying Lost Angeles patches.

The Mongolians had been birthed in L.A. due to most of them were Mexicans and the Lost Angels did not allow non-white members. The Lost Angels had flexed their muscle as the largest outlaw motorcycle club in the world and told the Mongolians that they did not have a right to exist.

The outcome of that was an ongoing war that is still happening today, some thirty years later.

When the Lost Angels saw our patches, they immediately went on alert and began to surround us.

Their leader then told us that we were not welcome in the town and that we needed to get on our tricycles and leave.

Neither Cut-throat, nor myself, were very good at taking orders from Lost Angels and we certainly were not going to allow them to dis-respect us or our club in public.

Cut-throat pulled out his Mongolian knife (Mongolians always carry huge knives, this is part of what we are well known for) and said, "Respect few, Fear none" (That is the Mongolian slogan) and began slicing and dicing. I of course joined in. We stood back to back and took on all nine of the Lost Angels.

When it was all said and done, the Lost Angels dragged their butts outside and got back on their bikes and into their cars and left. We knew that they would be back and most likely with guns so we headed out to the bikes. On the way out,

Cut-throat stumbled and fell. Upon closer inspection I determined that he had been stabbed in the abdomen and was bleeding profusely.

I had the bartender call an ambulance and they took him to the local hospital, where he died from the wound.

I now had to go back to the motor-home and tell his and my old lady what had happened.

She did not take it very well, and I was not very good at comforting her. My idea of giving comfort was to promise to kill every one of the men who had been involved with this.

As a result of the fight at the bar, about a week later, I was arrested for assault with a deadly weapon and sentenced to two years in the Texas Department of Corrections.

Three of the Lost Angels were also arrested for murder.

Neither them nor I testified or snitched on each other but there were other witnesses in the bar that did.

I found myself in a prison called the Wynn Unit in Huntsville Texas.

All of my experiences in the California juvenile system had well prepared me for this new environment.

I was as crazy as any man in this place. My first week in the prison, I was attacked by a black man and I tossed him off of the 4th floor tier of the cell block. He fell approximately forty feet and broke his neck upon impact.

The cops did not even complete an investigation on the death.

Later that week I was approached by the Aryan Brotherhood and asked to join them.

Chapter 4
1980

I was only doing a short two year bit but knowing me I would not get any good time so would have to do every single day of it.

The good side of that is that I would have no parole over my head when I got out.

I immediately opened up a two for one store, this is where I loan you one pack of cigarettes and you have a designated amount of time to pay me back with two packs.

I had found that this was a great way to make money and support one's self while in prison. It is a fairly up-front and easy business to get into.

There are some down sides to it though. For instance to run a two for one store, people must know that if they do not pay that there will be consequences.

One must also continually protect the store inventory or it will get ripped off while you are in the shower or day room. If someone rips you off, you had best have a plan in place to recover your goods and extend retribution to the offender.

Part of opening the store was that I had need of a couple of employees. It was my turn to help out the local economy by expanding the labor force of my business.

These guys would serve a couple of functions. One would be the collector and the other would be the protector of the goods. I of course paid them for their services.

One day I was in the day room playing a game of chess. I often played chess for money. I am very good at chess so it was not really gambling but rather charging them money for lessons as I was always going to win.

The guy that was playing me had placed three packs of Marlboro's up as a bet.

Apparently he had some issues with some other folks in the prison as a guy came up behind him while we were playing and slit his throat from ear to ear, spewing blood all over me and my chess board.

I simply stood up and looked the offender in the eye and asked, "Who's paying for a replacement board?"

He agreed to replace the board and we all walked away from the dead body. Such is the violent world in which I live.

They put me to work scanning microfilm for the Texas Department of Motor Vehicles. I worked five hours a day for ten cents an hour.

And people complain about minimum wage, how silly.

I was in this prison for about nine months when a riot broke out one day. I was in the mess hall when it went down.

You could feel the tension in the air. I had been through a couple of riots while at YTS, so I knew what was about to happen.

The difference was that here they were not using bean bag guns and rubber bullets, but rather real shotguns and rifles that would kill.

In a riot situation an inmate does not have many options. You can either join the riot or find a place to hide and there are not many places to hide. When the bullets start flying they are very indiscriminate and even those that are on the ground in compliance with the officers orders are subject to being shot.

I was watching the head honcho of the Black Muslims as he was the guy that was likely to kick this riot off. He walked over to one of the kitchen guards and hit him with a plastic tray across the face.

The protest was over bad food so good a place to start as any I suppose. When he hit the guard, simultaneously four other guards were taken down effectively giving these guys control of the chow hall. I was watching all of this go down, knowing that an army of cops was going to be flooding into the place in riot gear within minutes.

Fights broke out all over the building, food was being thrown everywhere.

Most of the whites (we only made up approximately 10% of the population) gathered into a corner so that we could protect ourselves as we knew that the blacks would be coming for us.

I am not a prejudice man but racial segregation is simply a way of life in prison. We did not have much in the way of weapons but were armed with forks, spoons and dinner trays.

A man came at me and he had a knife from the kitchen in hand. I was able to disarm him and in the process the knife ended up in his heart.

He should not have attacked me, huh. Here comes the goon squad. The guards came bursting into the room in full riot gear, tear gas had been deployed so we were all gagging upon it. Red dots were on men all over the building and batons were being swung profusely.

I hit the floor and interlaced my fingers behind my head and prayed that they would not shoot me.

When it was all over there were four inmates and two guards dead.

One of them had been by my hand. It was self defense but now I had to hope that no one saw who did it and gave me up as I would get a life sentence out of this action.

We all got corralled by the guards and thrown into a lock down situation for the next two months. No one ever questioned me about any of it, so I had gotten away with killing the man. No one cared!

The next year flew by pretty quickly and I was fast approaching my release date.

They offered a parole to me about eighteen months into the sentence but I turned it down, preferring to do the extra six months and have no parole when I got out.

The day of my release finally came. I was given $200 and a set of poindexter clothing.

They took me to the bus station and let me go.

I took the bus to Houston Texas where I caught a plane to Los Angeles.

My Mongolian brothers picked me up and we immediately went down to a check cashing store 43 and robbed it. I was back in action baby, time to party.

Over the next month I probably robbed fifty places in the Los Angeles area, and had a new Harley, and a truck.

I had found that many liquor stores also served as check cashing facilities for illegal's, and so began robbing them.

We hit a liquor store one night on Lankershiem Blvd. in North Hollywood. We had completed recon on the establishment and knew that there was a fixed shotgun under the register pointing towards where a robber would be and that there was also an armed guard in the cooler behind the milk, where he could see everything.

We walked in and one of my brothers went in the back while I was keeping the cashier busy and he took out the guard. I had conveniently positioned myself so as to not be aligned with the shot gun blast if it came. As my bro was taking on the guard, I pulled out a 44 magnum and robbed the cashier, including the check cashing 'kitty' that he kept in a special drawer.

We left the place with over $20,000 that night.

Another night, I was eating dinner at the Brown Derby restaurant in Burbank California with a new friend. This guy was really riding me hard wanting me to pull a robbery of some liquor store that cashed payroll checks. I did not know him well and did not trust him so kept saying no. He was hitting home and I was beginning to suspect he was a cop.

He kept pushing and pushing until he finally pissed me off. There were four cops in the place so I got up and went over to their table and introduced myself properly.

"Hi, my name is Rabbit. You gentleman need to each place your guns on the table in front of you, oh yeah, and get your handcuffs out too." I proceeded to disarm and rob the cops leaving them in their own handcuffs, then I robbed the restaurant and left my friend sitting there looking dumb founded.

I walked out the door got into a police cruiser that had the keys left in it and drove away. I drove about two blocks up the street, pulled a car over by hitting them with my police lights.

The car I was pulling over was a brand new Mercedes. There were two occupants, so I addressed them over the loud speaker and had them exit the car and spread eagle on the ground.

I love playing cop; folks do everything you tell them too without question. I emptied their pockets, wallet, purse, hand-cuffed them and placed them in the back of the police cruiser telling them that they matched the description of an armed robbery suspects.

I then left them there and got into their Mercedes and drove away with all their money. I drove the car to friends that had a chop shop in the San Fernando Valley, and sold it for $1,000 as is.

Chapter 5
Bonnie and Clyde 1981

I decided to go on a cross country crime spree again. This time it was just I and a chick that I had met, doing a Bonnie and Clyde thing.

This girl truly had no idea of what was ahead.

We took off from Los Angeles driving my old 64 Ford ½ ton with the Harley in the back end.

We decided to go to Las Vegas first. The trip to Vegas was a blast. As we roared down Interstate 15, we got drunk and high and partied down.

The gal I was with was named Michelle and she was a wild one for sure. She stripped down in the cab of my truck and performed every sex act in the book on me while I was driving. Once we got to Vegas, it was once again time to go to work.

We got on the Harley and headed over to the Show Boat Casino where we walked into the poker room and robbed the game for

$40,000 cash and hundreds of thousands in chips.

We took off from that casino and went straight to the Tropicana Hotel, where we did the same thing again.

This time we got $32,000 cash.

In those days the casinos were still owned by the mob, so we were indeed living dangerously but thought we were ten foot tall and bullet proof.

A fearless crew is a dangerous crew as if they have no fear, they are unstoppable.

We took the money and headed to the Sahara Casino where we lost $29,000 at the crap table. Easy come, easy go.

We were bold and fearless but not so bright sometimes. What made us think that we could rob two Vegas poker rooms and then go to another and gamble, without the mob finding out where and who we were, I have no idea.

In some areas, we were dumber than two rocks.

Six mobsters showed up packing really heavy. We reacted by not talking at all, we simply pulled out our weapons and opened fire.

I shot the one that had spoken to us in the forehead, killing him instantly. Bonnie meanwhile opened up with her pump shotgun that she had hidden in her skirt, cutting the second mobster literally in half. I then somersaulted across the room, shooting as I was flipping, killing two more of the mobsters. While I was doing that, Bonnie had cut two casino security guards in half.

Bonnie was turning out to be a crazy bitch. She was truly enjoying all of the blood and guts and was cackling and screaming at them to bring it on.

While Bonnie was doing her thing, I shot another mobster five times in the chest. I then dove under the craps table and flipped it over, while the last mobster unloaded an automatic weapon in my direction. When I heard his weapon jam, I jumped up and did a flip, landing about three feet from him. I spun around with my Mongolian knife in hand and literally cut his head clean off of his shoulders.

We left Vegas that night very quickly heading towards Denver Colorado we still had over $40,000 in cash in our possession.

On the way to Denver we robbed four different businesses. Most of them only netted around $500 each, but it wasn't the money anymore, but rather, the addiction and power of pulling a robbery that motivated us.

I'm sure that the mob was trying to track us as we had literally massacred their men, but we were going forward as though we owned the world and didn't have a care to worry about.

We were truly disillusioned and psychotic. Only a person who has entered into an armed robbery can understand. There is a rush of adrenaline that courses through your body, a power that is better than any drug, a feeling of euphoria that is as addictive as heroin. We got high on this and had to keep getting our fix.

We needed to keep our heads a bit low for awhile so I was exploring the idea of changing our profession to more of a white collar type of thing, but I was addicted, so could it really be done? While in Denver I discovered that one could take as much or more from a bank with checks as with robbing a bank.

You don't get the cool euphoric high like with a robbery but it is much safer and very lucrative. I made a decision to go after this as our main business and just pull armed robberies when we absolutely needed an adrenaline fix. You know how it is I had found an easy way to make money and was going to run as hard as I could with it, while still getting my adrenaline fix from pulling more robberies. You have got to remember that computers were not in use within the private sector in those days.

We met up with a guy that I had met in prison down in Texas by the name of Trigger. Trigger was a professional forger who provided us with some great fake identification and gave me a payroll check machine and lots of blank checks written on an active corporate account.

We sat down and figured out how to create our payroll checks and once we had it down, it was time to go to work.

We were going to cash these checks at super markets. Most stores, in those days, required that 10% of the check be spent on groceries, so we rented a U-Haul trailer and pulled it behind the truck so we would have a place to put all the groceries in the trailer.

After filling the U-Haul we would go and find where all the homeless folks were at and give them the food.

Like I said earlier, there were no computers. Therefore, the grocers could not consult a computer like they do today. The best that they could do was to call the bank and ask if the check was any good, and we had that covered too as all of our checks were written on real accounts that actually had the money in them, they simply were not our accounts.

We then sat down and mapped out every grocery store in a city before we hit it.

This allowed us to start cashing checks on Friday night and have hit every store in the area by Sunday night. It typically took a bank three days to figure out what was happening and put the word out that an account was not good any longer.

We hit Colorado Springs first. They had 27 grocery stores and our average check was written for $400, with a $350 take home amount. 27 x $350 = $9450. Hey $10,000 a week with no gun was pretty good money in those days.

We spent the entire summer going from town to town, cashing payroll checks, and partying down.

In the midst of this though we missed the euphoric high of pulling robberies so at least once every couple of weeks we robbed a business of some sort.

I had found that rent to own furniture businesses dealt mainly in cash and that on any given Friday they were likely to have at least $3,000 cash.

Therefore I had a tendency to rob rent to own businesses or liquor stores that cashed checks.

We spent most of the summer running checks and pulling robberies.

I really loved the folks in Utah as the Mormons there were so easy to rip off. It was as though they had turned the clock back 50 years and they were begging people to con and rip them off.

I soon found out that although these folks were a bit backwards, if they caught you stealing their money, they would give you a lot of years for your trouble. When it comes to Mormons, you can rape their women and children but do not mess with their money. The reason I say this is that in those days they only gave you 5 years for child molesting and/or rape, but if you stole their money, you got 15 years.

I was 25 years old and was now serving a couple of 15 year sentences for fraud and forgery in the Utah State Prison.

I had written and cashed payroll checks totaling over $300,000 in Salt Lake City using my own name.

I know that is pretty stupid but at that time I was young and dumb and simply didn't care. I was a walking crime machine in those days. I had a new car every day, stolen of course. I always had a pocket full of cash, due to I would rob, steal or con every minute of every day.

I was a very good looking young man and quite articulate. If you had money or something worth money that I could figure out a way to relieve you of, it was a done gig.

I also robbed drug houses regularly, robbed a few banks, and was a member of an outlaw motorcycle club named the Mongolians MC that manufactured crank (speed).

While in Utah State prison I was a member of the Aryan Brotherhood which is a white prison gang.

I had been a member since my days at YTS (youth training school), which is a youth prison in southern California.

My job was to collect debts owed to the brotherhood. How I went about doing this was up to me, all that mattered was that I got the money any way possible.

Typically I would purchase a debt from the brotherhood and then go about the work of collecting it.

If I did not get the cash, I lost money, and one cannot run a business in that manner.

I was transported one day from Utah State Prison to a local county jail in a small Utah city. I was informed that I was being charged with a forgery in their city.

I didn't even remember ever being in this town, but it was my modis operand, so it was probably me.

More importantly, this dump they called a jail was not acceptable to me. At the state prison, I had my own cell with a TV. and the chow hall was buffet style, not this hard jaw breaker that they called meatloaf in this jail.

I walked into the court and told the judge, "sir, I will plead guilty to felony forgery today and accept a 15 year sentence run concurrently with my other sentences, if you will guarantee that I will be returned to the state prison by tonight".

The judge accepted my deal and gave me 15 years run concurrently with my other sentences, meaning that it was a new conviction but I would not do anymore time.

I know I was truly psychotic fool.

One day I had purchased a debt in the amount of $300 from the Aryan Brotherhood. I paid them $200 and would collect $600 from the debtor.

Yes it is expensive to go into collections in a prison setting. The debtor was a Mexican guy that had made the error of purchasing drugs and cigarettes on credit and then did not pay the debt. I walked over to him during visiting and introduced myself in a very polite manner, to his wife.

I then told her about his debt and that if she did not give the funds to a friend of mine in Salt

Lake City by this time next week, I would break both of his legs and arms and that if she went to the authorities, he would die.

I worked jobs like this all the time and usually the loved ones came through.

If not, then I would make good on my threats or worse yet, sell the guy into prostitution.

To me it was just business. If I did not follow through on the threats, then that would become public knowledge and no one would ever pay up. I couldn't have that now could I?

This time, though, things did not go quite right. It turned out that the wife was a family member within the Mexican Mafia. She went to them and told them what was up and they sent word down through the system that I was to keep my hands off of the man.

If I did that, I would be out of $200, and my reputation would be marred, so that was not an option to me.

I walked down to his cell with a ball bat and began to tune the guy up and made good on my promises. When it was over, both of his arms and legs were broken, as I had accidentally broken his neck as well. He was dead.

I then soaked him and everything in his cell with lighter fluid and lit the cell on fire, walking away calmly down the tier, to my cell.

The entire prison was locked down for three weeks while the murder was investigated but no charges were ever filed as there was not a single witness willing to talk.

Imagine that in a prison full of snitches and rats, I guess no one wanted the same treatment.

For every action there is an equal or greater reaction.

The Mexican Mafia went to the Aryan Brotherhood and made a drug deal worth a lot of money.

The Mexicans would continue to sell heroin in the prison, but would step completely out of the speed, marijuana, and prostitution business.

Like our congress, they placed some pork into the deal. One of the pork add-ins was that the Aryan Brotherhood would turn their heads while the La Familia killed me.

I was warned by a friend on the counsel, and I couldn't allow that to happen, so I put a plan of escape into play.

I had already spent a couple of years planning how to escape from this prison and now it was time to do it.

Rabbit man is about to earn his name once again.

Escaping from a medium security prison is a tough thing to do but it can be done. Many attempt it and a few actually make it over the fences, past all the locked doors and gun towers but even fewer actually make it more than a mile from the prison before they are shot or captured.

I could not afford to have either of those things happen. I had some pretty good incentive though, as my pride would not allow me to check into protective custody, and yet I was smart enough to know that if I stayed in that prison, I was a dead man walking.

I had gotten married to a gal that was the sister of a fellow comrade in arms, i.e., another convict.

Yes, we met and married in the prison. She was a down biker chick so she would be willing to do what I needed her to.

The next week during visiting I told her the plan and attained her buy in. It was getting really hard for me in the prison now due to the hit on me and the fact that my prior brothers in the Aryan Brotherhood were starting to feel guilty and demonstrated it by letting me know whenever one of the La Familias hit-men were making a move.

I knew though, that I only had a few days to live. Can you believe those Aryan pricks? They threw me under the bus and stepped out of the way on a green light being placed on me and knew they were wrong and privately admitted it but none of them pricks would step up to the plate and help me.

Word had gotten out all over the prison that I was going to be killed, even the cops knew and had offered to transfer me to protective custody, but I declined the offer.

I decided to use this to my advantage. I had a friend stab me in the mid section of my body. It was a very precise wound that did not hit any vitals but was enough to have me transported to the county hospital in Salt Lake City.

I was using an old play from my childhood, when I had escaped from YTS.

On the way there, the Mongolians MC (not wearing patches of course) blocked the road and forced the ambulance to stop.

The cops that were attending to me were subdued quickly and I was liberated.

We rode off on our bikes and headed for Wyoming, where my girl had a place for us to hide for a few weeks.

Chapter 6
1984

I spent the next year on the run. During this time I traveled all over the Western United States, robbing from the rich, and giving to the poor, me!

One Friday evening we hit just such a business in a little town called Grand Junction Colorado.

This place was located on a corner of the main drag in town. We pulled up into the parking lot next door with a stolen Plymouth Fury.

Michelle went in first and cased the place, noticing that when the cash drawer opened for a payment that it was flush full.

She signaled me outside that it was a go, so I came in and pulled out my .357 magnum and informed the guy behind the counter that I would be relieving him of his funding.

A guy came out from the back and he had a gun in his hand, so I shot him dead in the forehead. I had not planned to kill anyone but it had now happened. I couldn't leave any living witnesses. Now I had to shoot the guy behind the counter too.

Worse yet, I was going to have to kill Michelle also, as she too was a witness to a capital crime.

I wanted to do that in a more personal manner though later on so I told her to get into the car.

We had gotten $5,939 from the robbery, but now we were going to have to haul ass out of that part of the country for awhile as there were two dead bodies back at that rent to own place.

We headed north to Wyoming. When we got up into the mountains of northern Colorado, we pulled over on a back dirt road and found a quiet place to camp.

During a great round of sex, I slit Michelle's throat with a razor knife as I was ejaculating into her, wow what a wicked sensation it was as she died.

I simply could not have a living witness to two murders, so she had to go and I am one sick puppy when totally in the flesh. I buried Michelle next to a creek where I thought she could see the fish jump for the next couple of thousand years and then headed up to Cheyenne Wyoming.

I was now not only an escaped prison inmate but I am also wanted on at least 2 murders.

At the time though I did not think that anyone knew who had committed the crimes or that anyone knew about Michelle being killed.

What I didn't know was that there had been a third person at the rent to own store and that she had clearly seen everything that happened.

There had also been a new fangled security system in the place that had taken pictures of us too. Not good.

While I was hanging out in Cheyenne a state wide search was going on in both Colorado and Utah for me.

I spent the next couple of days in Cheyenne chasing whores and getting drunk, trying to forget what had transpired back in Grand Junction and later with Michelle.

She is the one person that I had killed thus far that I truly had regret for; the regret was not in having killed her but in not having been able to spend more time with her before I did kill her.

After about a week, I decided to go down to Denver and see some friends.

What I did not know was that there had been an intensive man hunt for me going on for over a week already.

When I got to Denver, my friends acted really skittish so I asked them what was up.

They told me that I had been on the news all day long for a week now and that I was wanted on a triple murder over in Grand Junction and that there was a reward out on my head.

I turned the T.V. on and sure enough a report came on showing a picture of me and offering $10,000 for information on my whereabouts.

I took off from my friends and immediately stole another car as the one I had been in was on the news.

I was at a 7/11 and a guy left the keys in his 1984 Porsche, so I took it. Once again liberating from the rich and giving to the poor.

I drove the Porsche up into the mountains and found a small cabin to rent up close to Aspen Colorado. It was a little hole in the wall place where I might be able to lay low until these cops settled down a bit.

I had a wonderful fishing creek on the property so on my second day there I went upstream about a mile and caught some of the prettiest trout a person could ever see.

I was walking back to the cabin and saw that it was surrounded by police cars.

I had everything I needed to survive in the forest with me so I hoofed it into the hills and hid where I could see what was going on but they could not see me.

It took them three days to finally trap me in the mountains. These guys pulled out all the stops. There were helicopters, dogs, and an army of cops in those hills.

I finally got trapped in a bears cave and had nowhere to run, so I gave up and walked out with my hands high in the air.

Chapter 7
The Trial

I was taken to the county jail where I spent the next two years in a one man cell with no TV. no books, no clothes, not even a pair of underwear.

I had been charged with three capital murders and they were seeking the death penalty.

I didn't have any money to pay a lawyer because the cops had confiscated all of my money, and seized it as being illegal gains.

My lawyer was a state appointed dump truck that they called a public defender. This guy was so bad, that he advised me to just plead guilty with no guarantee of the death penalty being taken off of the table.

We spent many months going through the preparatory stage for the trial, me in my strip cell and the attorney doing whatever it was he did, which was not much.

When it came time for the trial that I had insisted on having, I was told by the judge in his chambers that I would be found guilty in his court and that I would receive the death penalty.

I was actually happy that he made that threat as I knew that it may be my only reprieve when it came time for an appeal on my conviction.

I understood that my attorney was not going to do anything to keep me out of the death chamber, and that I was going to need something, anything to keep that needle out of my arm.

As the trial progressed, my attorney did exactly what I had expected, nothing.

Whatever happened to the presumption of innocence anywise?

He knew that I was guilty and that the prosecution had a solid case, but, he never even explored such things as insanity, or anything else, he simply allowed the prosecution to run the show and heeded to the judges warnings and offered no resistance.

The actual trial lasted three days and the jury came in with a verdict in thirty minutes of guilty on all counts. They took another three months to complete psychological evaluations and obtain victim statements, etc and then they held a hearing to determine what my sentence would be.

I was convicted of three counts of capital murder and sentenced to death three times. I was then moved to DEATH ROW!!!!

Chapter 8
DEATH ROW

I had been in prisons in several states, and had spent literally years in solitary confinement, but nothing had prepared me for what I was going to experience emotionally when I entered death row.

This place was the last stop. One could not be placed any deeper within the prison system than this.

Every man in here was going to die.

Don't get me wrong, all of us are going to die, but most do not know the exact date and method of death, these men do.

There were 138 other inmates on the row and we were all sentenced to death. All were going to die and although every one of them had very tough exteriors, inside we were all scared little boys.

We just couldn't let anyone know. Wow, I have hit the big leagues now. There is no parole from this place.

I really had a hard time wrapping my head around these facts.

I was placed in a cell and informed that I would be in my cell 23/7 for the next six months. I was allowed out one hour a day for exercise and showering.

There were 18 men in my pod and only one of us was allowed out of our cell at a time.

I was not allowed visits, phone calls, or any type of outside contact.

After the first six months, I was finally moved to the general population of death row.

We were still locked up most of the time, but I was now allowed one hour a day to intermingle with three other death heads.

This was always interesting as all of us are psychos, that's why we're here.

The first time I entered the day room, one of the other three came over and asked, "Are you my new road dog?". I answered by stabbing him five times with a toothbrush that I had fashioned into a knife.

Dealing with these guys had to be majorly violent as they are all cold blooded killers. He lived, but wouldn't be asking me anymore stupid questions.

I was sent back to isolation and spent the next five years in a cell with no other inmate contact other than the trusties that brought food around.

After a few months, they began to allow me to order books from the law library so that I could prepare my appeals.

I spent the next ten years learning the law and filing appeal after appeal. I attacked every possible avenue that I could find, but the one that would eventually attain a change in my sentence came back to that conversation in the judge's chambers, but we will get more into that later.

I had been on the row for about two years and during that time I had not only studied the law but also had read the Bible no less than 200 times, cover to cover. My exposure to the church as a child had made it where even though I may want to believe what I was reading, it was difficult, as I had a deep hatred for religious people. And more than that, how could a holy God allow such things to have happened to me, or allowed me to do the horrid things in which I had done?

I had a lot of things to work out in my head. But one thing for sure, I had become extremely knowledgeable in the Word of God, if not yet a believer.

One day I had just finished reading the book of Acts and had a revelation. Suddenly the Words were jumping out at me and making total sense to me. I began to understand that maybe this Jesus dude really could change and fulfill me, just maybe.

I spent a total of twelve years fighting my appeals.

One day the guards came down and told me to roll it up. Huh? Why? Where? They told me to shut up and do it, so I did.

I was transferred to the main prison and placed in a holding cell.

After about five hours, an attorney came into the cell and informed me that I had won my appeal and was being taken to a re-sentencing hearing that very day.

I was taken to court and the same judge that originally sentenced me, changed my sentence to three life terms run consecutively.

This meant that I would never see the light of day again but that I would live my life out in the prison until I was either killed or died a natural death.

Chapter 9
2008

For those that need a recap. I am now serving a triple life sentence in Colorado State prison. The case that I am here for was an armed robbery of a rent to own store that went bad and ended with three people being killed.

I was convicted of all three murders and the robbery.

I was initially sentenced to death, but that was later commuted to three life sentences without the possibility of parole.

Bottom line is that I have already been here for 26 years and I will die here. Oh, and if I were to ever get out of here, I still have two, fifteen year sentences in Utah to complete.

I will never get out of this place, and to be honest, I don't deserve to.

It's all cool, I earned my place here and have a proven violent nature, I really don't ever belong on the streets again, as I would not even know how to do the most basic things in life and would most likely re-offend. I do not want that to happen so am perfectly happy serving God right where I am at.

I spent 13 years on Colorado's death row. It is amazing how much one can reflect upon their life while sitting in a 6x9 isolation cell for 13 years.

For several years the only reading material I was allowed was a Bible. I read it over 300 times, cover to cover.

One day I decided that I certainly had nothing to lose by accepting Jesus into my heart so I got upon my knees and repented of all my sins. I clearly understood that repentance did not mean saying the words "I'm sorry", but rather an acknowledgement that what I had done was wrong and a willingness to turn away from such and never do it again. I laid them all before God and asked Him to come into my heart and set me free from the sin that consumed me.

I asked Him to release me from the insanity that I had been living in for so many years. I promised Him that I would spend all the days of my life being as much like Jesus as I could. Not religious, not like what I call churchianity, not a fake religious child molester like Pastor Dick, but rather walk, act, talk and do like Jesus did.

I had spent many years mad at God for what folks like Pastor Dick, had done to me. I blamed Him and hated him as a result. But now I had come to realize that it was not God who had done these atrocities, it was not Him who had beaten me as a child, it was not God who had ordained these tragic events, it was man, who had fallen into the depravity of sin.

I did not do as so many do, and ask God to get me out of my situation as I knew that I deserved to die for what I had done.

All I wanted was to know that I was forgiven of my sin and that when I did die I would go to heaven.

The Word of God says in John 3:16 "For God so loved the world that He gave His only begotten Son so that whoever believes in Him shall have eternal life." I embraced this scripture and stood upon it and trusted it to be true.

Over the next ten years I studied the Bible sixteen hours a day and applied as much of it as I could to my life. I never asked God to get me out of my death sentence but I did commit to Him that I would serve Him no matter what until the day I died.

When my sentence was eventually overturned, I praised the name of Jesus, and made a pledge that I would serve Him all the days of my life by leading others to redemption via being like Jesus.

As I entered general population of the prison I began to preach the Gospel of peace to all that would listen.

What is preaching the Gospel of peace to all?

I asked that myself, and what God showed me was that Jesus healed the sick, made the lame walk, the deaf hear, the blind see, the dead rise. He also set the demoniacs free, He turned water into wine (try that one in a prison setting, you will be extremely popular. Loll), walked on water, fed thousands with two loaves of bread and a couple of fish and He raised the dead, oh did I already say that.

I found that there was a group of believers and joined them. Being that I was never going to get out of prison and had such a solid knowledge of the Word of God, it was not long before I became a leader in the church and the men began to call me pastor.

On my third visit to the chapel joining in for a Sunday morning service, I stood up and walked over to a brother that was in a wheel chair. He had been shot by the police and was paralyzed from the waist down. I laid hands upon him and commanded his body to be healed in Jesus name. He stood up, fully healed and not only walked but ran and leaped. I asked him to go and show the cops and see what they said.

He was taken to the hospital where they ran many, many test on him and determined that he had indeed been healed better than new.

Once the word had gotten out about this miracle, other came and I began to lay hands upon them too, and they were healed. One man was a gimp and was not anymore, another was blind in one eye and now he sees, another was healed of a bad back, another was healed of deafness, and then there was the blind man.

I laid hand on all that came and prayed over them and they were healed. The Chaplain was a non-believer with a Methodist background that simply had a great state job, but didn't believe in Jesus, so the men had never looked to him for leadership.

He and I bumped heads real hard as although I loved Jesus, I was not very subtle sometimes and I told him he was an old non-believing heretic.

Suddenly I was transferred to another prison. No warning, no reason given, but I trusted God as He is in control of all things.

I as a professing Christian am much different in my beliefs and actions than most any organized church one might find out in the free world. Rather than being encumbered by history and tradition, we were able to form a belief system that closely parallels that of Jesus ministry.

No politics, no formal rules, except for one. I began to preach Do What Jesus Did!!!

What did Jesus do? He healed the sick, made the lame walk, made the blind to see, raised the dead and provided a path by which we as sinners and transgressors of the law can traverse through the spilling of His blood in order that my sins may be forgiven.

He paid the price so that I would not have to. It is my duty as a Christian to live as much like Him as possible and spread the great news of His redemptive power.

I am now 52 years old and have racked up a total of 36 years behind bars.

It started as a kid in juvenile hall and then progressed as an adult. At this point I am totally institutionalized and would not be able to function in society.

Yes, even though I am a tongue talking, devil chasing, Holy Ghost filled, Fire baptized man of God, my calling is right here where I am at, in this prison being employed by the Holy Ghost to set the captives truly free.

I am a John the Baptist type preacher that is on a mission field no other can actually enter into and live.

I have a prison ministry like no man since Paul the Apostle

Many wonderful men and women of God are involved in prison ministry but none of them have the ability to be a true missionary and live amongst the indigenous population.

They all have to leave every night and will always be foreigners in a land they cannot truly understand.

I live in a maximum security prison where the worst of the worst live and grace is abounding in ways that would blow your mind.

We are in the midst of a true Holy Ghost Revival in this prison.

You see, the prison that I was transferred to is run by a warden that is a Christian and he likes what he sees happening here.

They do a security count of all inmates five times a day, so we have to plan our church activities around the count.

We began having church in the prison yard a few months ago, but never had a clue as to what was going to happen. Firstly let me define what I mean by the term "church". To me the church is the living ecclesia, i.e., people who gather together to worship their creator.

This is not a formal organization but rather a living organism that cannot be controlled by religious fools that preside over denominations from hell.

Yeah, I know, I am still a rebel at heart, but one that walks to the best of my ability as Jesus did and shares the great news with all that will listen.

When we have church it is a time where the Holy Spirit is welcome to do as He chooses to do. He heals the sick through the hands of His servants, He sets the demoniac free as they convulse upon the ground and then arise a new man set free by the power of Jesus name. Prophetic utterance is a normal occurrence in our services, as well are baptisms, laying on of hands, fire falling from heaven and prophetic toungues with interpretation, feeding the hungry (yes even in prison there are the rich and the poor), and what I call walking on water which in this case is the fact that the guards never disturb our meetings even though we are in clear violation of the rules.

Our Bible study began with a group of ten men. It was actually pretty simple; we just got together and began to sing praises to God and study out of the book of John. Next thing we knew, men began to show up in droves as the healings piled up.

Everyone wants to either be or see a person healed miraculously, even hard core convicts.

I quickly began to get nervous that the guards would shut us down as we were not allowed to have large assemblies in the yard and we have over 200 men showing up to these meetings.

Why are there so many people transforming into the church in this prison? Because God is moving and setting the captives free.

Miracles began to happen, a man who could not hear suddenly was hearing.

Another man suffered from a bum knee and it was healed.

Another one couldn't read and he suddenly had the ability to read from the Bible but could not read anything else.

Some of the worst of the worst in Satan's castle are falling on their knees before a Holy God and repenting of their sin and allowing Jesus to transform their lives.

We are presently doing four meetings a day. I have instructed the men that they are only allowed to attend one meeting each day, and have assigned times for each to attend.

I am doing this to keep the guards happy about the assembly thing. We are getting away with things that are simply not allowed in a maximum security setting but our warden is a born again believer in Jesus, so we have been given a wide latitude.

Warden Jessup had an encounter with God that had changed his life and he had spent years fighting the local churches for funding to try and start a revival in the prison system, only to find that it was all politics and most of the elders of the local churches really didn't care.

The warden had made a decision to step up to the plate on his own and began backing our move to evangelize our world.

We are now six months into this revival and the Spirit of God is pouring out all over this place. Approximately 70% of the prison population now attends our Bible Studies.

I am literally teaching from morning to night every day. Men's lives are being transformed and changed and bodies are being healed every day.

We even have guards now coming to the Bible Studies. They come under the guise of crowd control and security but they too are believers that have actually volunteered to come on during their off work time to attend.

Even the warden has come to our meetings. He has pretty much given me carte blanche on running meetings as the violence in this place has dropped drastically, as well as other offenses.

The warden believes that we are having a true Holy Ghost revival on level with some of the greats of the past like the Azusa Street revival in 1905.

Today I am preaching on the subject of abundant living. The message God gave to me for these men is that they do not have to wait until they get out of prison to begin living an abundant life.

Men are rising up all over this prison as great warriors of God. They are laying hands on the sick and they are healed. They are casting out demons and setting the captives free. They are creating miracles all over this place every single day.

I love you Jesus as there is nowhere else in this world that I would rather be than right in the midst of your Holy Ghost Revival, not only in our prison, but across the entire prison system, and to the utter ends of the earth.

We follow a simple rule of thumb, act, think and do like Jesus did.

As men are transferred to other prisons, they carry the revival with them. Men that are released are being considered missionaries being sent from our church to that of the free world.

As a result there are no less than 13 churches now in existence on the streets of Colorado. It gets better, it really does.

From the church in our prison, missionaries have been sent into prisons within 32 different state prison systems and 185 United States cities, and 14 other nations.

Walking as Jesus did is the simple answer to all truths.

Turn the water into wine, don't trip on whether it has alcohol or not, as that is not your problem, it is God's. If He chooses to do anything He does, who am I to argue with the one and only Living God?

I can imagine now, you the reader at home, yeah you, the religious self righteous one saying, he's advocating drinking alcohol. No I am not, I am advocating that God can do what He so chooses and that neither you nor I have a right to question Him on it.

In a five year period we have seen a major revival break out not only in the prisons but around the world.

Don't let anything human or demonic keep you from becoming what God has called you to. If He has placed a dream in your heart, a vision to accomplish, a challenge for you to overcome, then walk in it my friend and allow God to employ you in the manner in which He desires, not you.

As for me, well, I am going to spend the rest of my life in this wonderful place and I am also going to see thousands led to Jesus and churches will be planted literally around the world from right here at Colorado State Prison.

How about you at home? Have you repented of your sins and allowed Jesus to take over the leadership of your life? If not, you need to do so right here and now.

List out your known sins to God, tell Him everything, He already knows anywise. Then go and sin no more, rather choose to follow Jesus.

Choose to be like Him.

Chapter 10
2010

It has been many years now since I gave my heart and life to Jesus. Since those early days of revival some truly miraculous things have transpired.

Proverbs 29:13 says, "Where there is no vision the people perish".

As we sat here in Satan's Castle we spawned a vision. One that was far beyond ourselves, as we were lowly convicts, how could we possibly touch a dying and lost world with the Great News of the death and resurrection of our savior?

And yet we have.

The warden set up a video conference this week where I am able to deliver a message to churches worldwide that have spawned from our revival here in Colorado.

I am told that there will be over 150,000 people viewing my message live and countless others on the internet later.

They fitted me with a headset microphone that you can't even see, it is really cool. There are several camera people here from an international Christian station filming what I have to say.

Wow, what a trip, me a convicted killer serving a triple life sentence without possibility of parole, and yet, I am the leader of a major worldwide movement of God.

God's grace is indeed sufficient!

Action….. "Where there is no vision, the people perish" and I am here to tell you that where there is vision, the people prosper.

If you will dare to dream big dreams, you can attain them.

If you will dare to repent of your sins, a Holy God will forgive you and put you in your proper place within the Kingdom, even if you are in prison.

If you will dare to lay hands on the sick like Jesus did, they will be healed.

If you dare to walk, talk, and act like Jesus, you will overcome any storm.

If you dare to raise the dead, they will rise.

If you dare to turn water into wine, you will be the life of the party.

If you dare to place mud in the eyes of the blind, they will see.

If you dare to cast demons out of the afflicted, they will be set free.

You see folk, we must learn to be like Jesus. Can we manufacture His deity?

No. But we can do what He did and even more, He said it, not me.

We can lay hands on the sick and they will be healed, we can lay hands on the blind and they will see, we can cast out the demon of cancer and pray and the damage done to the body, ravaged by that demonic disease will be healed.

It has nothing to do with our economic or social status. God can use anyone.

He often chooses to use the lowliest of life to confound the wise. He chooses to employ folks such as myself that have been the most despicable of all humans.

He chooses to employ us to accomplish great things that are impossible for us in the flesh but through the Spirit can be done.

I am told that hundreds of thousands of people will be viewing this broadcast today.

Ten years ago I sat on death row awaiting my execution. I even came within three weeks of it at one point before God intervened.

Now I am serving a triple life sentence with no possibility of parole, ever, and yet God has chosen to employ me to ignite a worldwide movement of walking like Jesus and doing what Jesus did.

Why does God choose to use those such as me? Is this unusual for Him? No, it is not. All through history, God has chosen to use those such as myself.

Moses was a murderer and yet God used him to lead the Israelites.

Saul was a mass murderer of Christians and yet God chose to use him to take the Gospel to the Gentiles and write 1/3 of the New Testament as Paul the Apostle.

God is not a respecter of men. He uses those in who He chooses to use and He can do it under any circumstance.

Do not ever allow the enemy to steal your dreams. If God has placed a dream in your heart, follow it, no matter what.

God told me in a dream many years ago now, to walk as Jesus did and do things exactly the way I saw Him do them.

He directly told me not to play church but rather to do what Jesus did. I therefore set out upon a study of the actions and words of Jesus and I found that what he did was heal the sick and set the captives free, therefore, that is what I do.

I was on the prison yard last night and a man was brought to the Elders of our church. He had been stabbed three times with a prison shank. He was going to die if a miracle didn't happen right now. He was lying there, bleeding profusely still, and we, the Elders laid hands upon him. As we began to pray the flesh miraculously healed before our very eyes. He was as though he had never had a wound. I then simply told him go and sin no more, just as Jesus had told the woman brought before him for adultery.

This man got up, felt all over his body and found no wounds. He then fell upon his knees and began to repent of his sins and hand his life over to Jesus, lock, stock and barrel.

That folks is what the church is supposed to be all about. It is not about getting rich. It is not about who has the fanciest car. It is not about who has the most perfect doctrinal statement or theological seminary.

It is about being like Jesus and doing what He did, setting the captives free.

In a few short years we have seen this great move of God explode worldwide and I am presently speaking to people in 40 countries, maybe more.

I could not have possibly imagined this even a few years ago and yet I was not afraid to step through the doors the God opened to make it possible. Why? Because I have a vision! My vision is to take the message of "Do What Jesus DID" to the peoples of the world.

If Christians would quit playing church and start doing what He did, they could not contain the crowds within their walls.

If ministers of God's Word would dare to get out of the way and allow God to flow through them and employ them to set the captives free, they would find that their churches would be meeting at the local NFL football stadium due to lack of room anywhere else.

Catch this vision folk; understand what it is that I am saying to you today.

Know that if you will dare to walk as Jesus did and start laying hands on the sick and raising the dead, if you will dare to cast out a demon or allow God to use you as a prophet (remember these folks are not usually popular, they all got stoned back in the day), or as a home Bible study leader, or worship leader. If you will simply step out to fulfill your vision of being like Him, He will empower you to succeed.

Think about it, I am in a maximum security prison and yet here I am speaking to you live via satellite. Amazing, absolutely amazing.

In spite of the fact that I was convicted of triple murder, God has given me a platform where I can tell you all how much He truly does love you and how much He desires to overflow you with an abundance of spiritual gifting.

He has done it within the walls of this prison. He has done it within the walls of prisons throughout the world this past year. He has done it in many of your lives already.

Perhaps you are attending this video conference with a friend and you have not yet made that step, breaking out of your box, but you desire to. I am here to tell you today that no matter how sinful your past has been, no matter how goody two shoes you have been, no matter what atrocities you have committed, God loves you and He already died for your sin.

All you have to do is accept Him as your Lord and Savior and repent of your sins, then move forward allowing Him to cultivate the gifting that He had already placed within your very DNA before you were even conceived.

All you have to do is step out on the water and walk.

How do I do that you may ask, simple, study up on what Jesus did and then go and do it, that simple.

I challenge you now, go and do what Jesus did. But you say, Pastor Rabbit, I tried all that. I laid hands on a sick guy and he died. Then I went and laid hands on a blind man and he went deaf. Then I told a demoniac that they could be set free and they committed suicide right in front of me.

To you I say, it is not up to you or me to decide who and where God will heal, it is ours simply to obey and trust Him to do it.

Be not deceived, it is not you or I, even a little bit. We are simply the vessels by which God chooses to move.

I had a friend that thought he was called to a healing ministry and placed himself in the path of several hospice patients. He laid hands on them and they simply died. He was confused. God, why? Why does everyone I lay hands on die? And then God spoke to Him this simple thing," they are healed son, they are with me."

This profound revelation opened this man's mind and heart and he now has a thriving ministry of assisting people leaving this world with dignity. What are you saying preacher?

I'm saying that each of us has a special gift that God has given us. For some that will be healing, others prophesy, others miracles, others prayer, others hospitality, and yet others the gift of redemption.

There are many gifts and Jesus demonstrated every one of them. Find your gifting within His walk. Study Him and find where your special gifting lies and then take it up and walk forward. No excuses. You can't tell me, uh well, I can't accomplish this because..... No, I won't accept that and neither will God.

I am serving life in a maximum security prison and yet I am able to touch a dying and lost world for Jesus, what's your excuse free man?

Do you truly desire to see and be a part of a true Holy Ghost Revival? Then begin to do what Jesus did, and the multitudes will come to you, even if you are on the side of a mountain, just like Jesus when He did the Sermon on the Mount. Go and do what Jesus did!!!!!

Cut.......

Everyone here at the prison is going nutz. They told me that the ratings on this live broadcast were 10 xs higher than expected. They say that 1.5 million people tuned in live.

Wow..... I headed back to the cell block and found that every TV. in the place had been watching me live and a cheer went up when I entered the building.

Even the hardest of cons in this place seems to love me these days and more importantly they are being blessed by Jesus because they are observing a history changing revival in their midst. Even if they do not yet understand, it will stick with them for the rest of their lives.

I don't know if this revival will go on forever, but I do know that we are presently right in the center of the inception point and that I am going to keep fanning the flames so that as many people in this world can be affected as possible.

We continued the daily meetings in the prison yard and God continued to poor out His anointing upon us.

We started a discipleship school that is an intensive course designed to give a convict an equivalent of a four year Bible College education but more importantly with a discipleship aspect that teaches them to act like Jesus did.

One day I was in the chow hall and a new guy was sitting at my table. He was angry that I had prayed over our meal and told me to shut up. I asked Him if he had a problem with God, and he hit me.

He clocked me pretty good too, right in the jaw and it caused me to fall out of my seat. Now everyone in the chow hall was watching and per normal prison protocol, I had to respond.

I got back up and sat down and began to tell him how much the Jesus that I know loves him and how he too could have the happiness that I had.

He hit me again I got back up and sat down again and told him that Jesus said that when someone hit you to turn your other cheek.

I then told him that I had done so and that I had no more cheeks to turn so please do not persist in attacking me.

He hit me again, or rather, he tried to. I caught his fist in mid air and broke his arm in two places.

Then, while he laid there in immense pain, I laid hands upon him and asked God to heal his body and bone came together with bone and he was instantly healed.

This guy's name was Daniel and he instantly became a believer and apologized profusely for his actions and much like Saul became Paul and changed his ways instantly, so did Daniel.

Daniel immediately joined our discipleship program with the intent of one day preaching the gospel in the nation of Egypt, his home.

Daniel was only doing a five year stint so we would only have him in this facility for a very short time and therefore must accelerate his training and preparation as we are going to directly send a church to Cairo Egypt from this prison.

It's perfect. The government is going to deport him upon release and he has a heart for his people. We are already making contact with a church in Cairo that is willing to host him and assist him in starting a brand new church from scratch.

The response to our broadcast was immense. I was literally blown away at the reports coming in from all around the world.

People were doing exactly what I told them to do in countries all around the world and as a result miracles and healings are being reported from all over the globe.

Worldwide revival is breaking out in a big way. They say that over 300,000 people showed up to a meeting in Prague, and 284,000 in Geneva, and another 499,000 in Milan. Where miracles abound, people will flock by the thousands, just as they did with Jesus.

So why don't more people teach this?

Hmmm maybe it is the root of all evil $$$$, I'm not influenced by it so I see the Gospel in a manner that is much different and thereby am able to present it in a way that people understand and accept. Stick around for the next book and we will see where God takes this revival.

CPSIA information can be obtained
at www.ICGtesting.com
Printed in the USA
LVHW100841200123
737510LV00003B/103

9 781105 652752